3 4028 07914 0621
HARRIS COUNTY PUBLIC LIBRARY

W9-AMO-661

$16.99
ocn747534324
01/17/2012

SEISMOSAURUS

ZIGONGOSAURUS

APATOSAURUS

T-REX

ALLOSAURUS

IGUANODON

STEGOSAURUS

PTERODACTYL

NOTOCERATOPS

DINOSAUR
MARDI GRAS

By Dianne de Las Casas
Illustrated by Marita Gentry

PELICAN PUBLISHING COMPANY
Gretna 2012

*For my brother, Gary, and his Jurassic James Krewe,
a chomping, stomping fun family!*
—Dianne de Las Casas

*To Mom and Dad, who love parades and
know how to let the good times roar!*
—Marita Gentry

Copyright © 2012
By Dianne de Las Casas

Illustrations copyright © 2012
By Marita Gentry
All rights reserved

*The word "Pelican" and the depiction of a pelican
are trademarks of Pelican Publishing Company, Inc.,
and are registered in the U.S. Patent and Trademark Office.*

ISBN 978-1-58980-966-6

Printed in Singapore
Published by Pelican Publishing Company, Inc.
1000 Burmaster Street, Gretna, Louisiana 70053

Around the corner and down the street
The dinos move to the mambo beat
All the great big beasts are out
Getting ready for the parade route

DINOSAUR MARDI GRAS, CHOMP! CHOMP!
DINOSAUR MARDI GRAS, STOMP! STOMP!

Down in New Orleans

party!

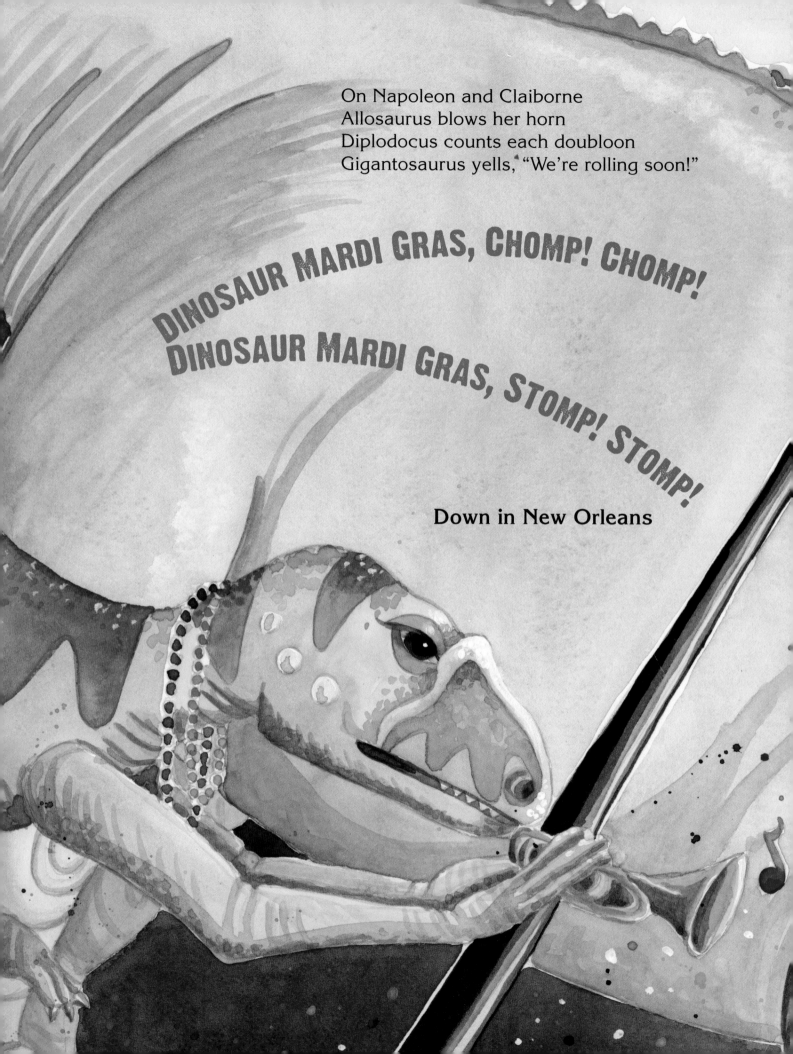

On Napoleon and Claiborne
Allosaurus blows her horn
Diplodocus counts each doubloon
Gigantosaurus yells, "We're rolling soon!"

DINOSAUR MARDI GRAS, CHOMP! CHOMP!

DINOSAUR MARDI GRAS, STOMP! STOMP!

Down in New Orleans

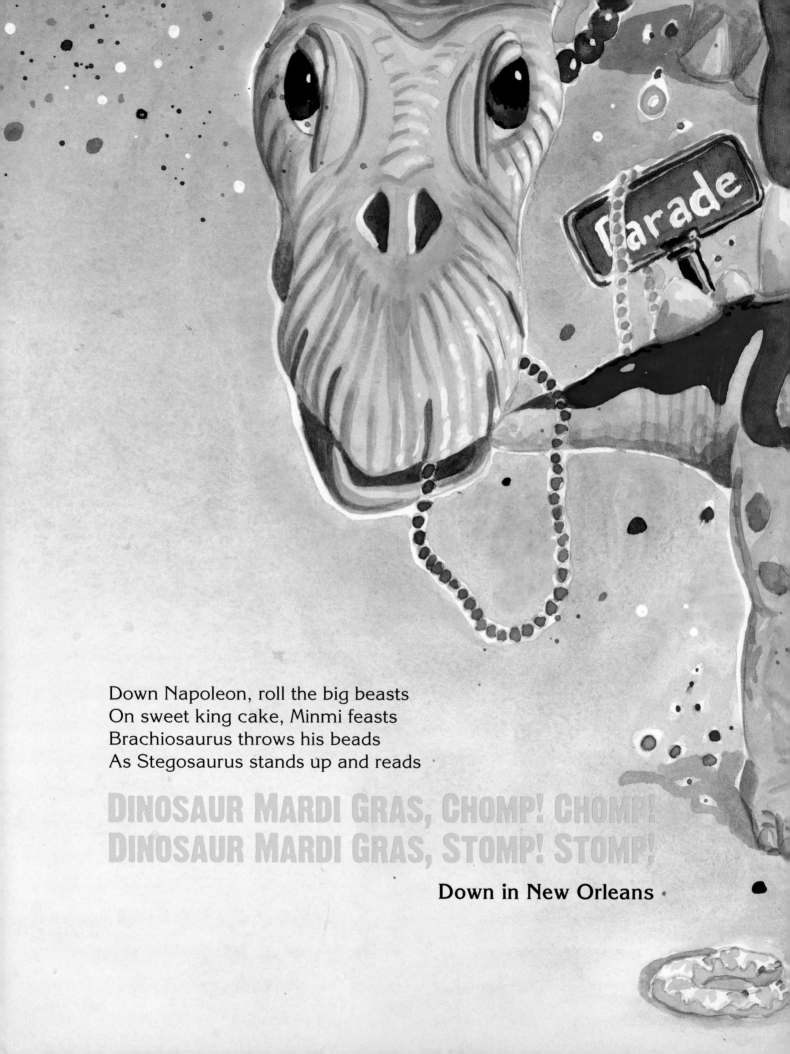

Down Napoleon, roll the big beasts
On sweet king cake, Minmi feasts
Brachiosaurus throws his beads
As Stegosaurus stands up and reads

DINOSAUR MARDI GRAS, CHOMP! CHOMP!
DINOSAUR MARDI GRAS, STOMP! STOMP!

Down in New Orleans

On St. Charles, the huge crowd roars
To see Rex, King of Carnivores
Pterodactyl swoops into the crowd
They love the parade and cheer so loud

DINOSAUR MARDI GRAS,
CHOMP! CHOMP!
DINOSAUR MARDI GRAS,
STOMP! STOMP!

Down in New Orleans

Around Lee Circle, they boom and bop
In front of the Grand Stand, the dinos stop
The mayor toasts the King of Dinosaurs
And the crowd goes crazy when T-Rex roars

DINOSAUR MARDI GRAS, CHOMP! CHOMP!

DINOSAUR MARDI GRAS, STOMP! STOMP!

Down in New Orleans

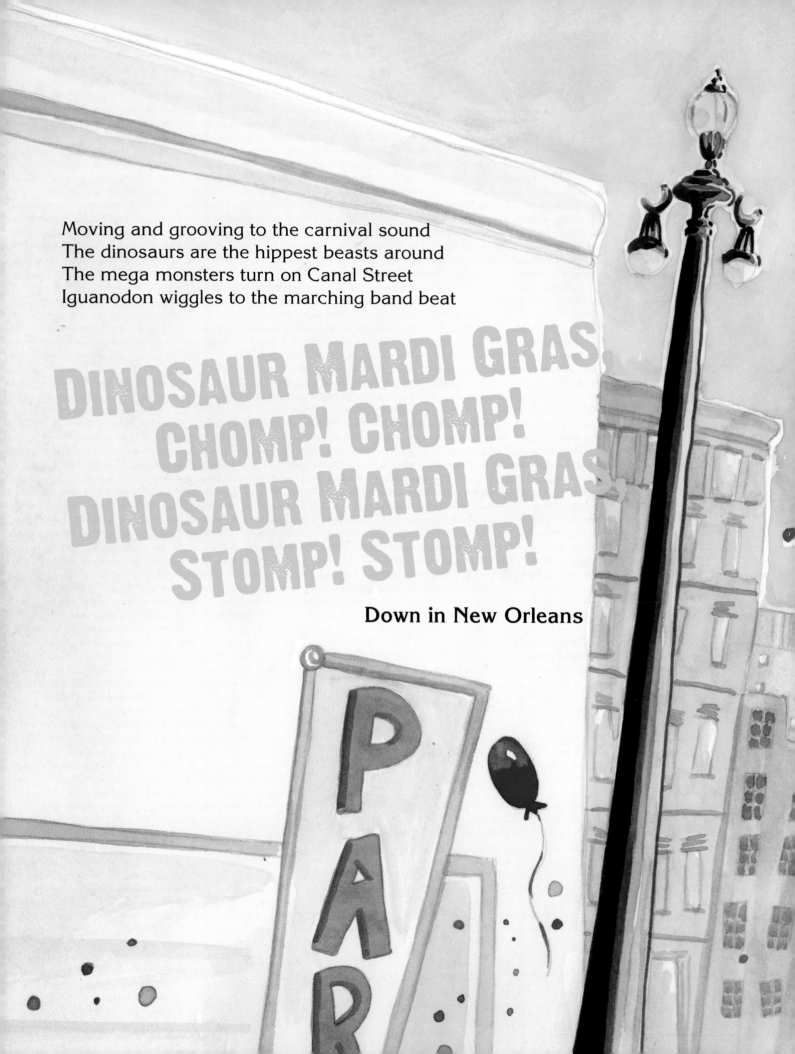

Moving and grooving to the carnival sound
The dinosaurs are the hippest beasts around
The mega monsters turn on Canal Street
Iguanodon wiggles to the marching band beat

DINOSAUR MARDI GRAS,
CHOMP! CHOMP!
DINOSAUR MARDI GRAS,
STOMP! STOMP!

Down in New Orleans

Oviraptor carries bundles of throws
Apatosaurus boogies while he's on the go
Pteranodon spins and soars around
The crazy creatures love to party downtown

DINOSAUR MARDI GRAS, CHOMP! CHOMP!

DINOSAUR MARDI GRAS, STOMP! STOMP!

Down in New Orleans

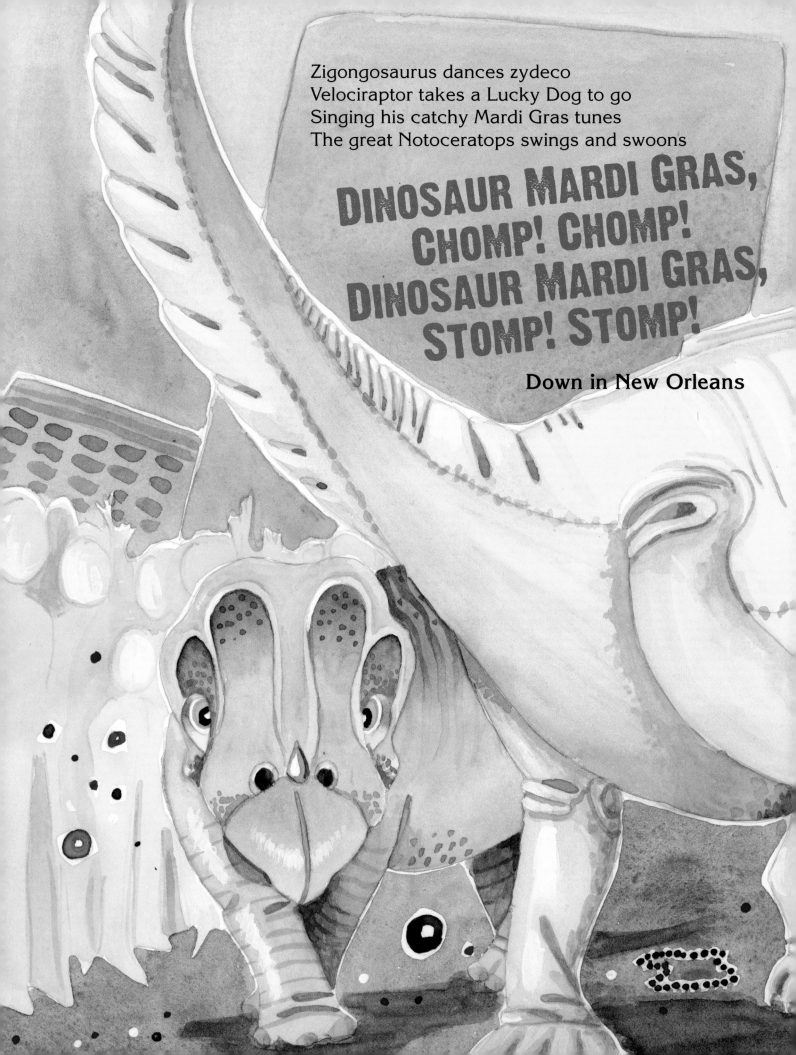

Zigongosaurus dances zydeco
Velociraptor takes a Lucky Dog to go
Singing his catchy Mardi Gras tunes
The great Notoceratops swings and swoons

DINOSAUR MARDI GRAS,
CHOMP! CHOMP!
DINOSAUR MARDI GRAS,
STOMP! STOMP!

Down in New Orleans

Passing Magazine and nearing the end
Big Seismosaurus makes a friend
Triceratops stops and sings the blues
Spinosaurus taps in his blue suede shoes

DINOSAUR MARDI GRAS,
CHOMP! CHOMP!
DINOSAUR MARDI GRAS,
STOMP! STOMP!

Down in New Orleans

Spectators gather in awe of the view
Beads fly from the floats of this motley krewe
"Throw me something, mister," the crazy crowd roars
And everyone hails the King of Dinosaurs

DINOSAUR MARDI GRAS, CHOMP! CHOMP!
DINOSAUR MARDI GRAS, STOMP! STOMP!

Down in New Orleans

T-Rex waves goodbye until next year
The happy crowd chants a carnival cheer
It's a jumping Dinosaur Mardi Gras
Hooray for all the jaws and claws

DINOSAUR MARDI GRAS,
CHOMP! CHOMP!
DINOSAUR MARDI GRAS,
STOMP! STOMP!

Down in New Orleans

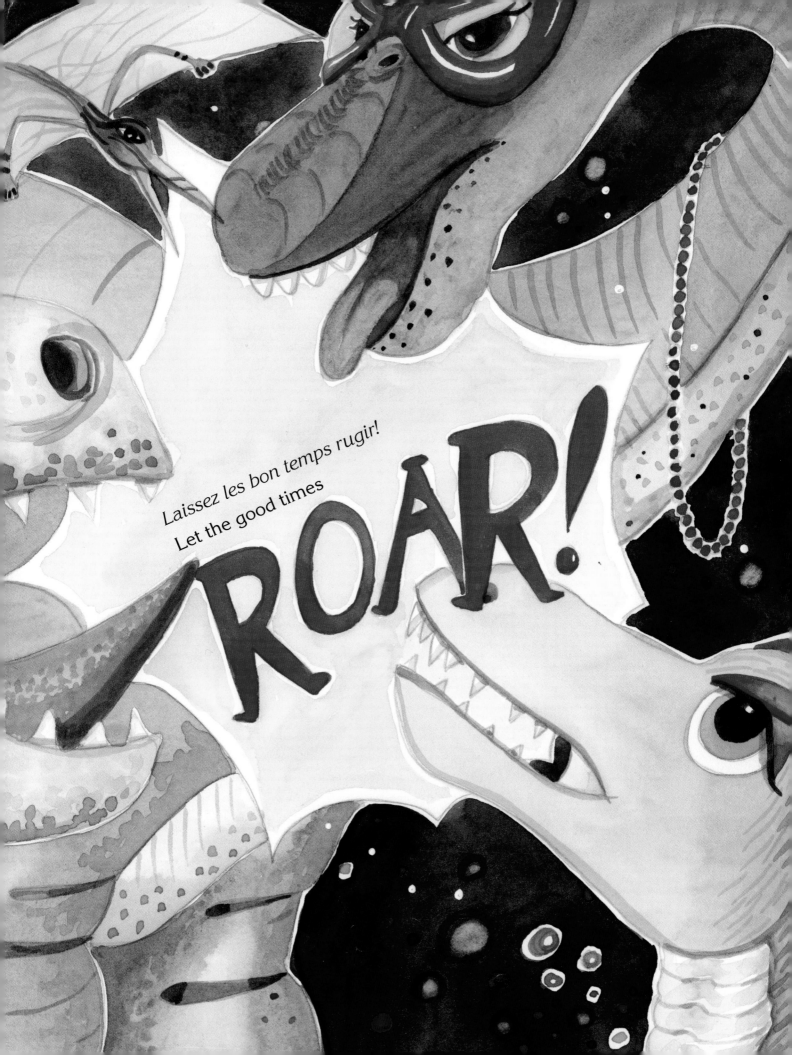

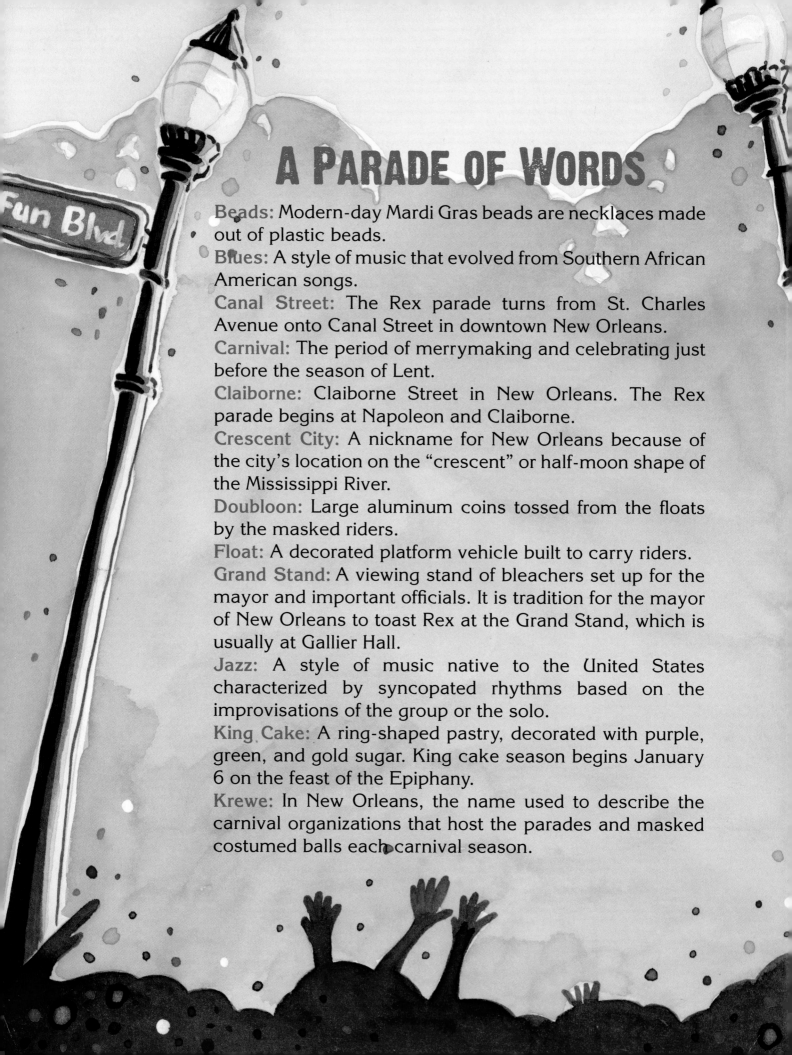

A Parade of Words

Beads: Modern-day Mardi Gras beads are necklaces made out of plastic beads.

Blues: A style of music that evolved from Southern African American songs.

Canal Street: The Rex parade turns from St. Charles Avenue onto Canal Street in downtown New Orleans.

Carnival: The period of merrymaking and celebrating just before the season of Lent.

Claiborne: Claiborne Street in New Orleans. The Rex parade begins at Napoleon and Claiborne.

Crescent City: A nickname for New Orleans because of the city's location on the "crescent" or half-moon shape of the Mississippi River.

Doubloon: Large aluminum coins tossed from the floats by the masked riders.

Float: A decorated platform vehicle built to carry riders.

Grand Stand: A viewing stand of bleachers set up for the mayor and important officials. It is tradition for the mayor of New Orleans to toast Rex at the Grand Stand, which is usually at Gallier Hall.

Jazz: A style of music native to the United States characterized by syncopated rhythms based on the improvisations of the group or the solo.

King Cake: A ring-shaped pastry, decorated with purple, green, and gold sugar. King cake season begins January 6 on the feast of the Epiphany.

Krewe: In New Orleans, the name used to describe the carnival organizations that host the parades and masked costumed balls each carnival season.

Lee Circle: The part of St. Charles Avenue named after General Robert E. Lee, where a statue of General Lee stands in the midst.

Lucky Dog: A famous mobile hot dog stand in New Orleans, found all over the French Quarter.

Magazine: Magazine Street in New Orleans. Rex passes Magazine on the parade route.

Mardi Gras: Mardi Gras is French for "Fat Tuesday." It is the last day of carnival.

Napoleon: Napoleon Street in New Orleans. The Rex parade begins rolling at Napoleon and Claiborne.

Rex: Rex is the King of Carnival, and his parade rolls on Mardi Gras day. Since 1872, he has been the symbol of Mardi Gras royalty.

St. Charles: St. Charles Avenue in New Orleans. St. Charles is the longest part of the Rex parade route, where thousands of spectators line the street waiting for the parade to pass.

Tchoupitoulas: Tchoupitoulas (pronounced chop-ih-TOO-luhs) Street. The Rex parade ends at Tchoupitoulas in downtown New Orleans.

"Throw me something, mister!": A traditional cry by parade spectators begging for Mardi Gras goodies.

Throws: Any goody that is thrown from a Mardi Gras float—beads, doubloons, plastic cups, trinkets, stuffed animals, etc.

Zydeco: In south Louisiana, a popular music that combines French dance melodies, African rhythms, elements of Caribbean music, and the blues.

Mardi Gras Shoe Box Float

In the New Orleans area, it is tradition for schoolchildren to build Mardi Gras floats out of shoe boxes. Make your float roar with creativity!

Materials:
Shoe box
Paint
Glue
Beads, sequins, or other decorations

Directions:
Paint or spray paint your shoe box and the shoe box top in a color of your choice. Turn the shoe box upside down and glue the top to one end of the shoe box, creating a backdrop. The rest is easy. Decorate! Use your imagination and create a Mardi Gras sensation. *Laissez les bon temps rugir!* Let the good times ROAR!

Author's Note
This story was inspired by my nephew's Mardi Gras shoe box float. The float had an erupting volcano and several dinosaurs on it. It was named "Jurassic Mardi Gras."

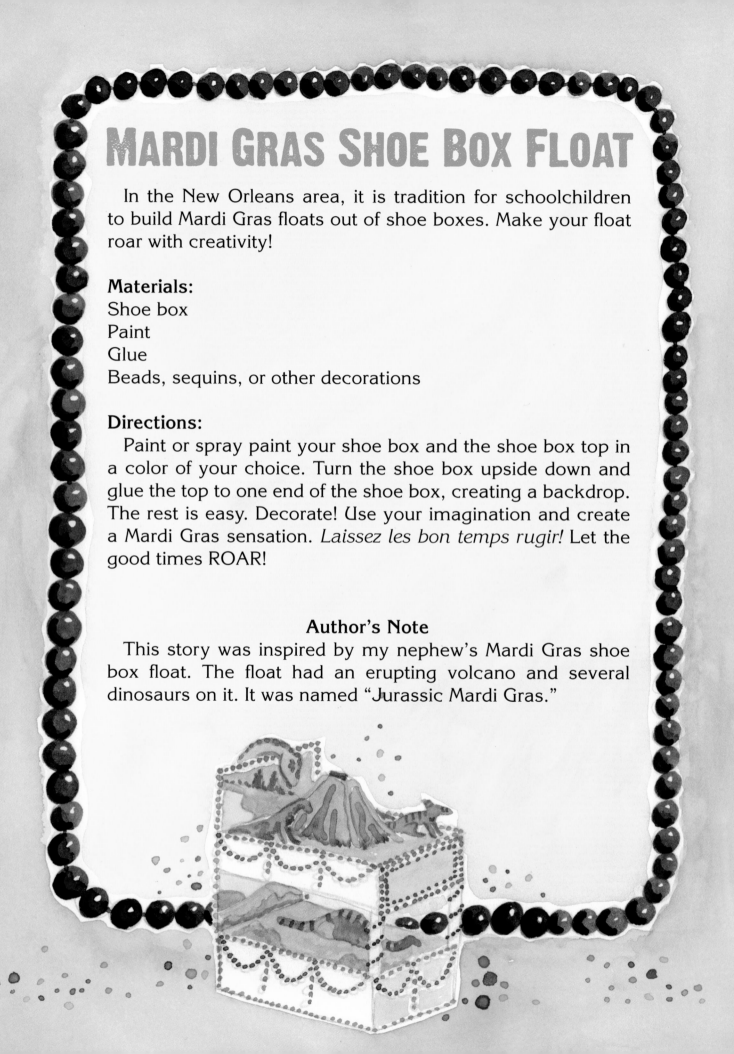